# Provence Sketchbook

*The City of Fountains*

**Anna A. Ryan**

# Provence Sketchbook : The City of Fountains



**ISBN-13:**
**978-1539514053**

**ISBN-10:**
**1539514056**

THEATRE
OPÉRA GRAND AVIGNON
OPÉRA GRAND AVIGNON
OPÉRA GRAND AVIGNON
VILLENEUVE EN SCENE

HOTEL
Salon de Thé
Restaurant Buffet
THE 2006 PRE-
LUCIE AWARDS
COCKTAIL

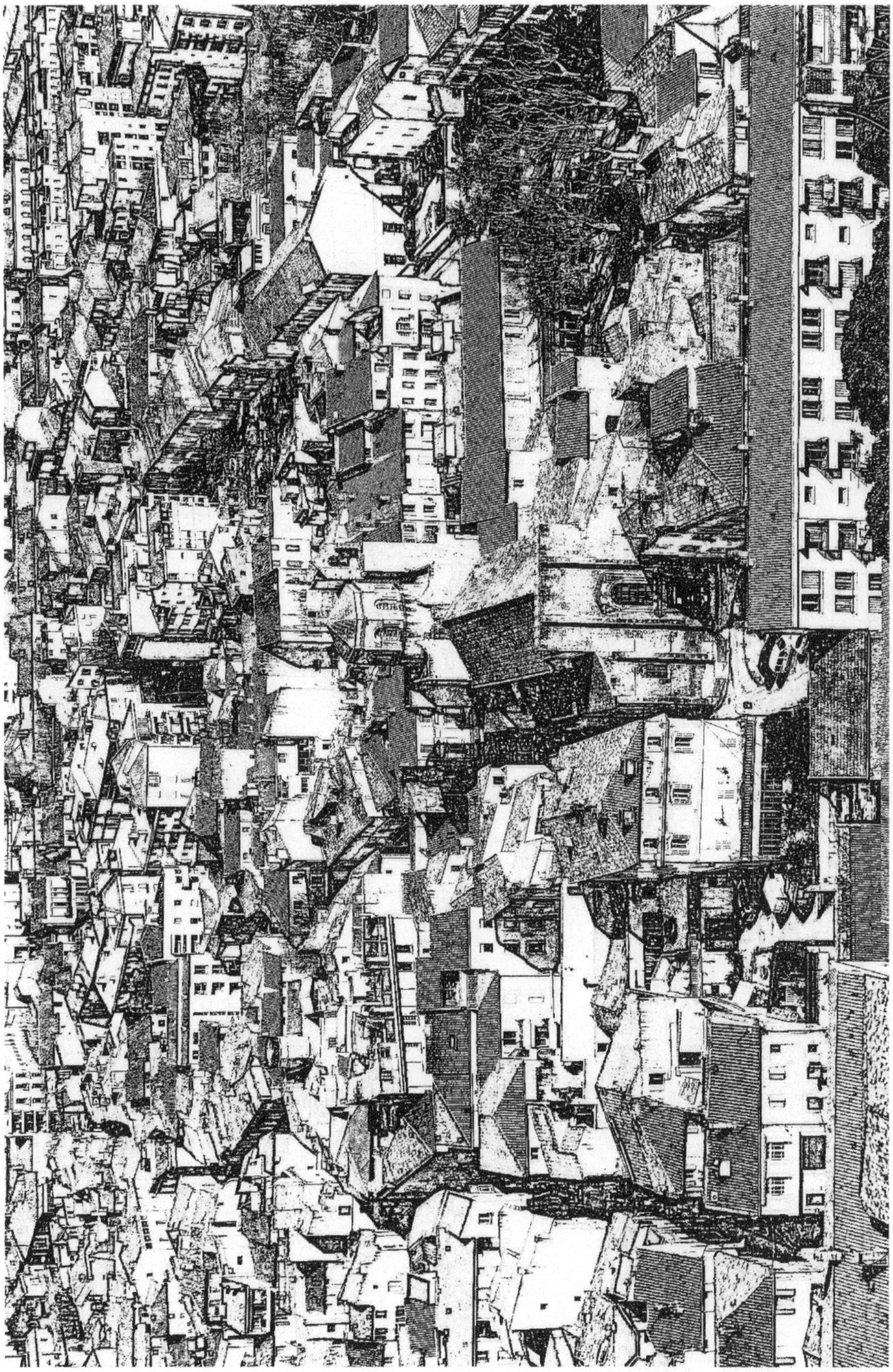

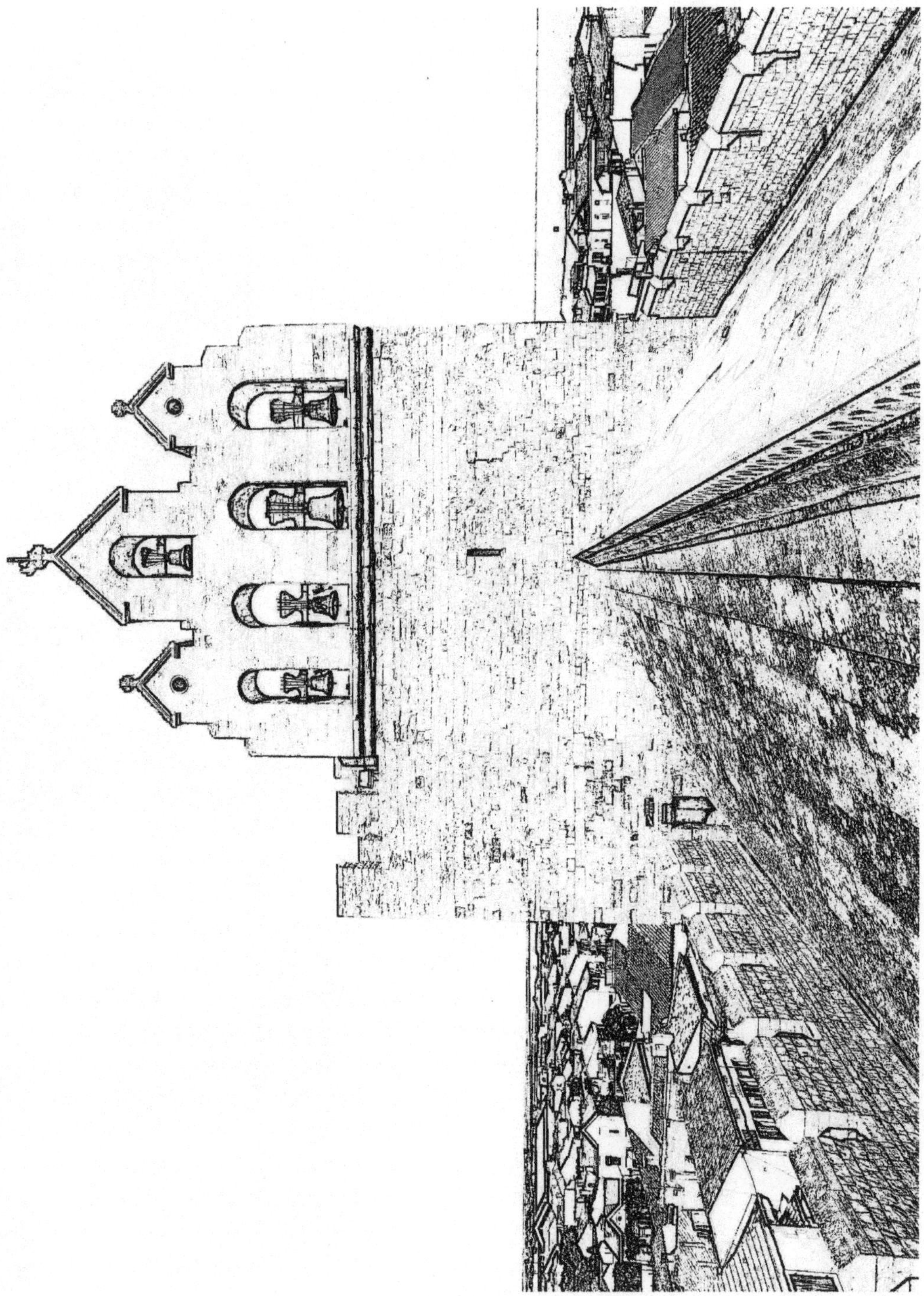

A CASA
A CASA
CAVE A VIN
L'EPICERIE...
OPTI

BRASSERIE
PIZZERIA
RESTAURANT

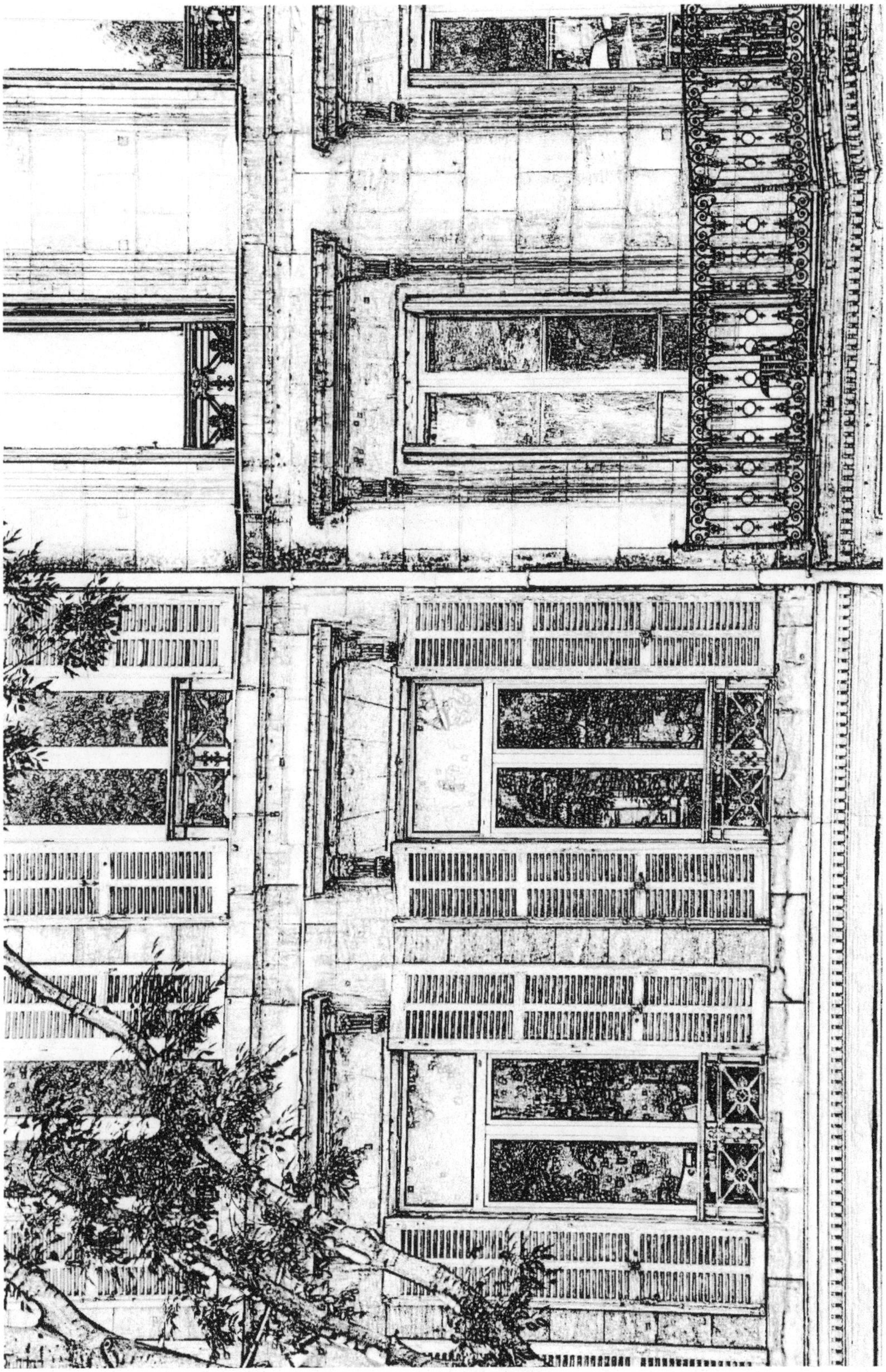

A VENDRE
SUGGESTION
MARMITE
23€

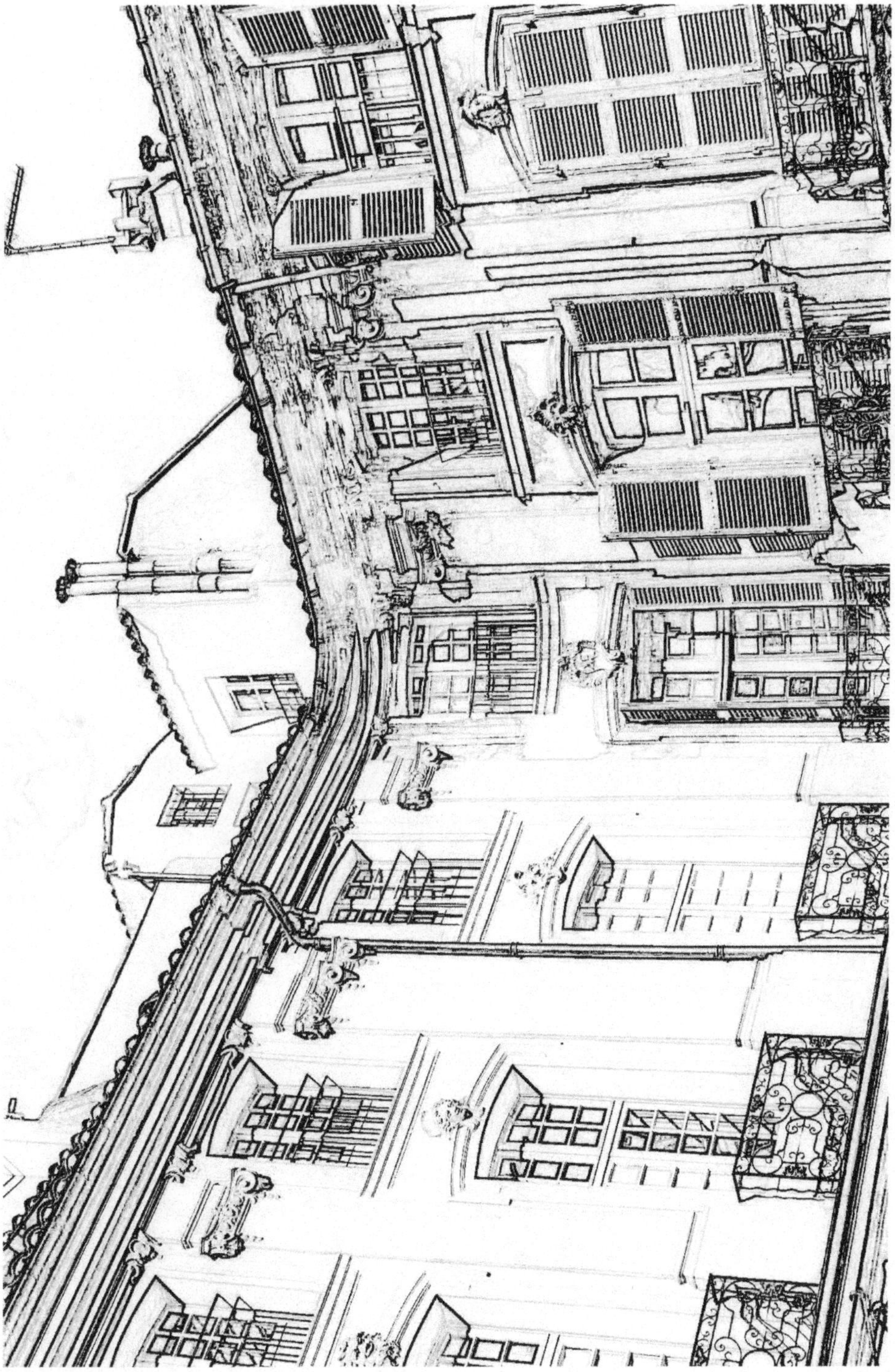

AUX MANES
DE LA PATRIE

CAVERIE
RESTAURANT
LA BROCHERIE
SENTOSA

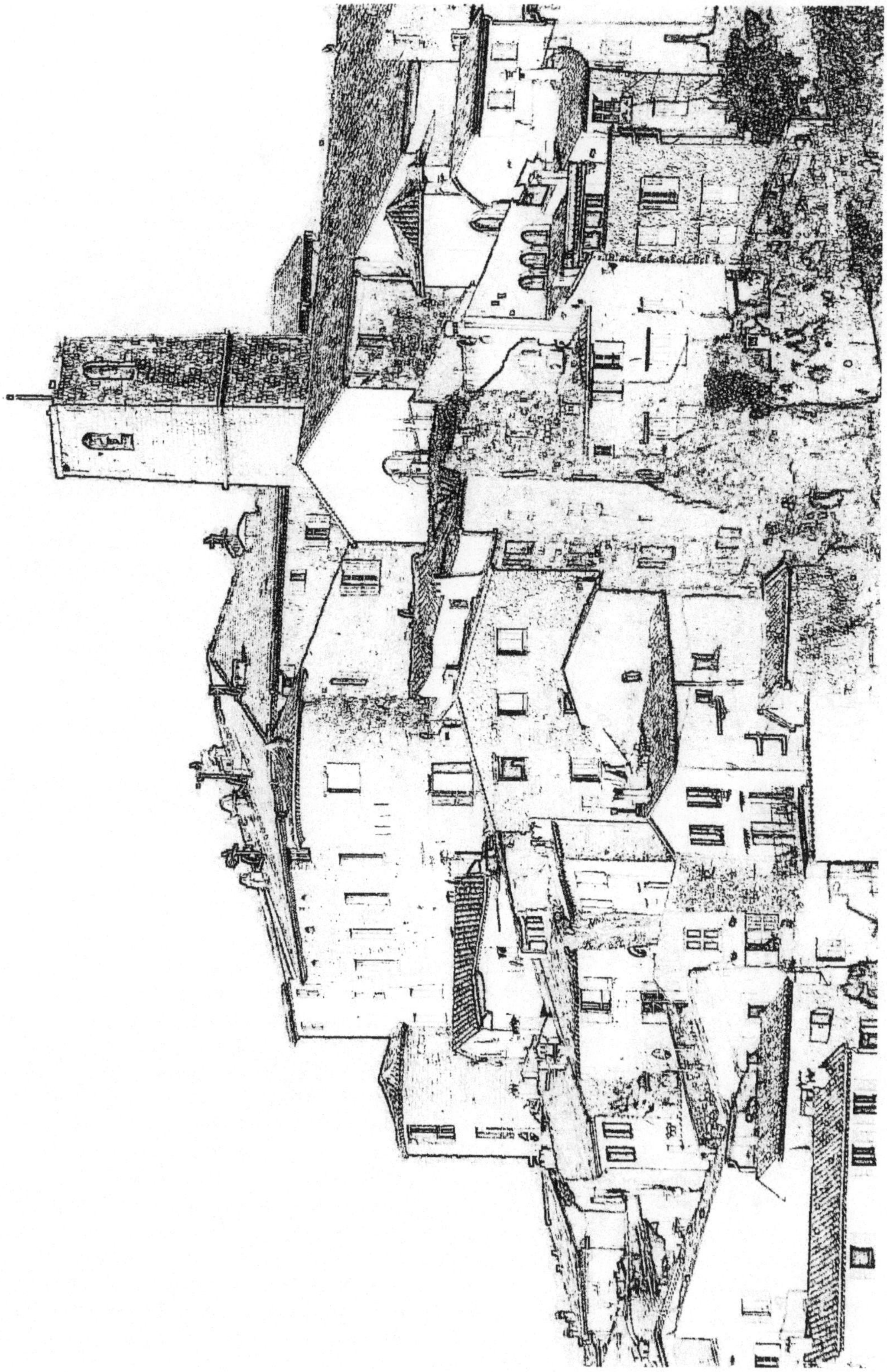

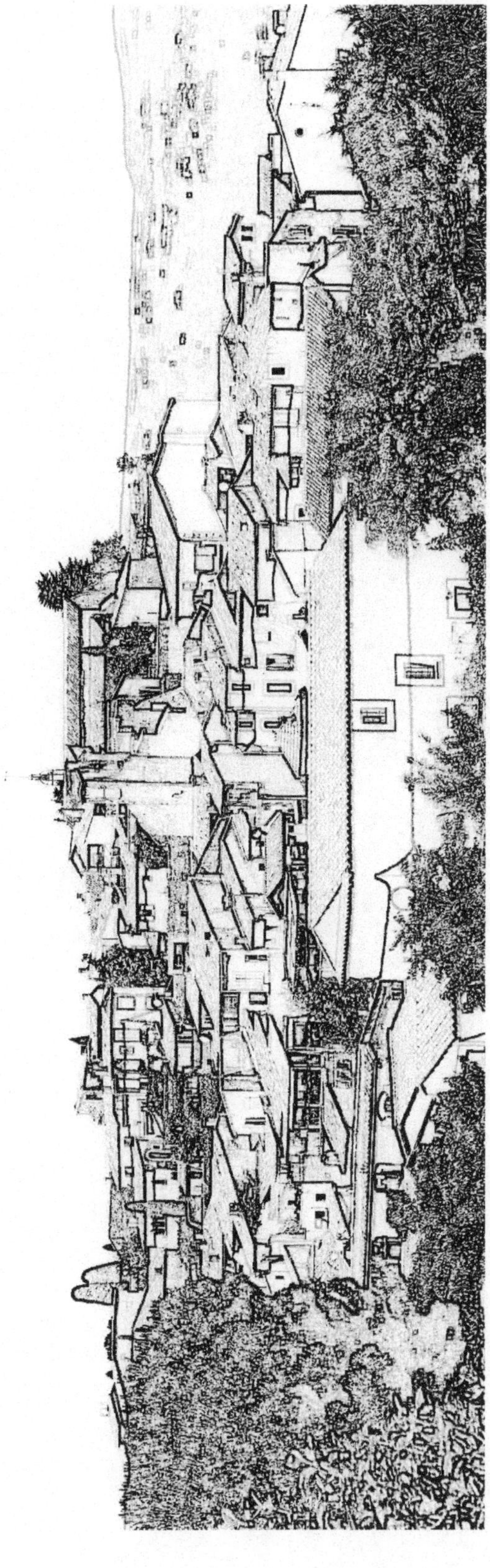

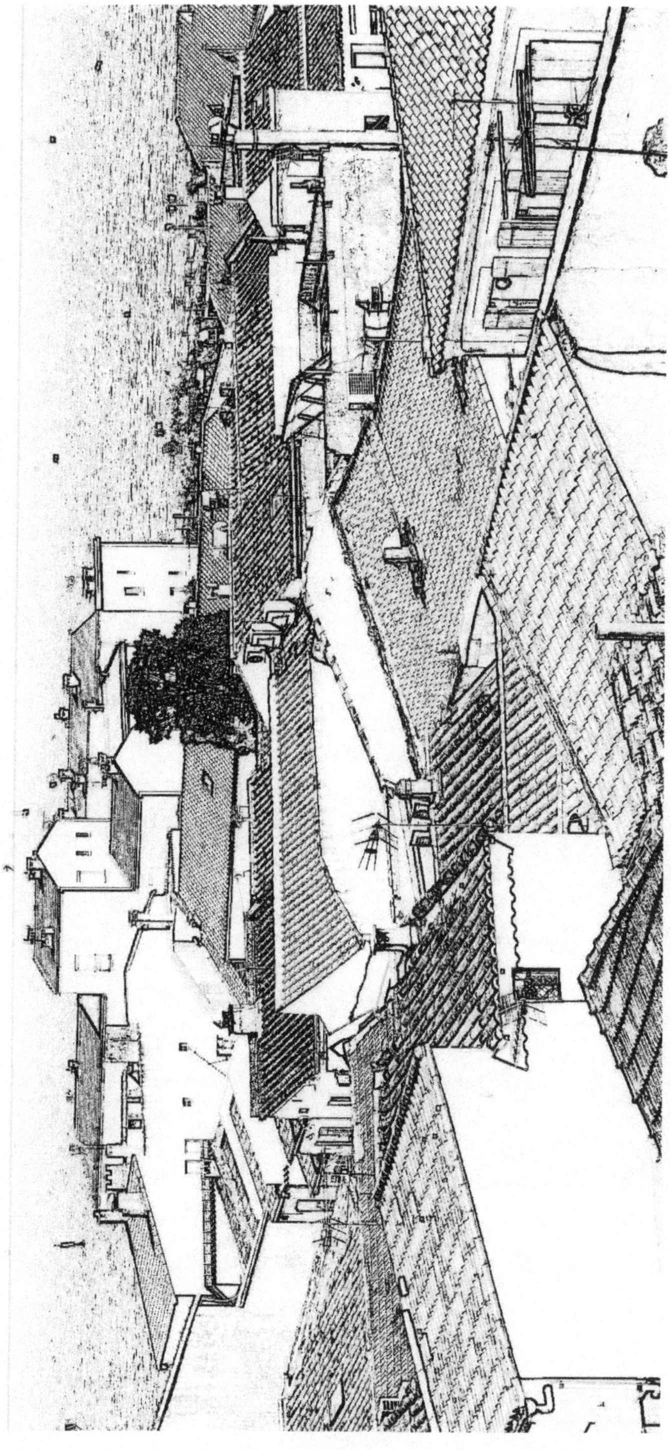

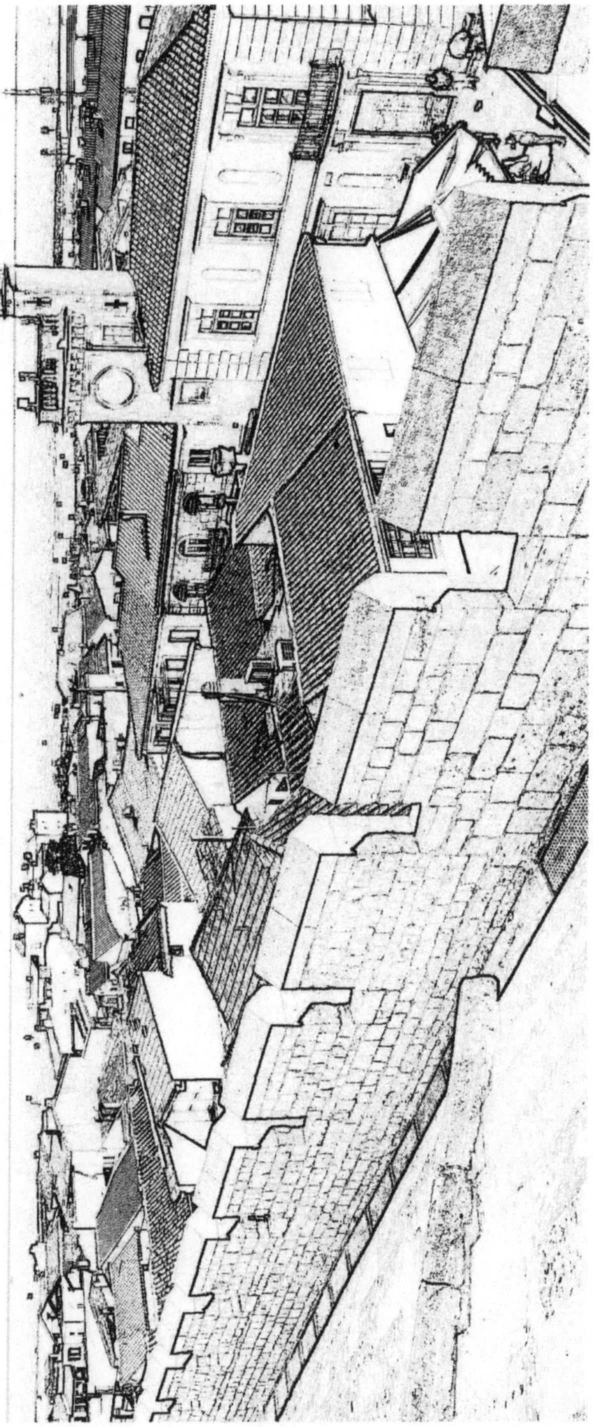

BRASSERIE

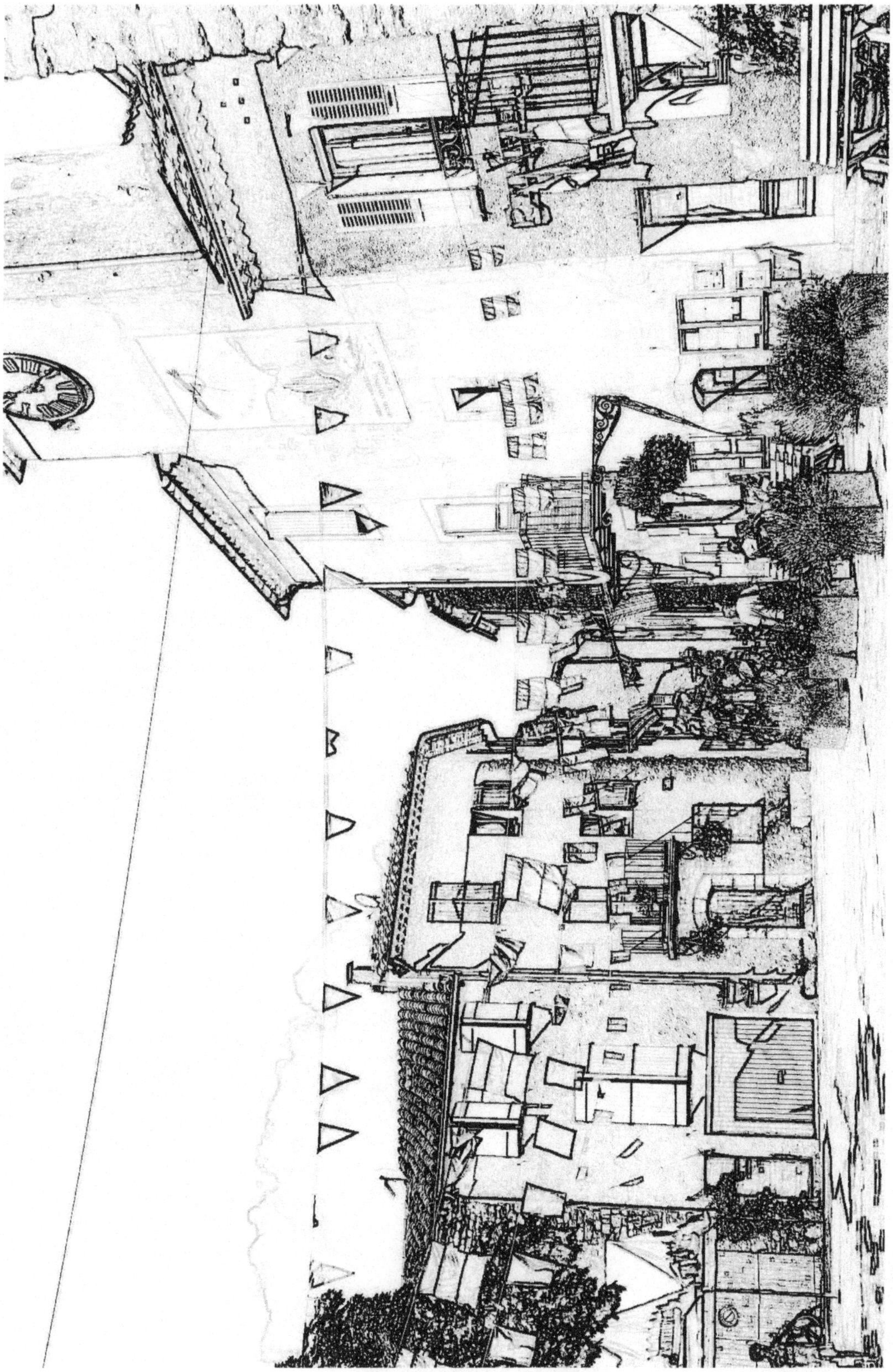